Stephei

Uncle Steve's Redneck Anthology

Volume 1

PublishAmerica
Baltimore

ISBN: 1-4241-0567-6
PUBLISHED BY PUBLISHAMERICA, LLLP
www.publishamerica.com
Baltimore

Printed in the United States of America

Dedicated to my ninth grade English teacher, Mrs. Valerie Gee.

1

GOOD TO THE LAST DROP

C'mon, gimme another round," Jim Varner said as he slumped over the bar counter, and loosely sat on the bar stool.

"Jim, you've had enough for tonight, why don't you take a rest?" The bartender suggested.

"That's the same thing my ex-wife said...and now we're divorced, gimme another round," Jim insisted.

"Okay, it's your life, drink it away if you want." He passed Jim another beer. "Thank you, I will." Jim began to drink slowly. He slid off the chair every now and then and would scoot himself back up, he was a true to life alcoholic.

Jim was just a loser that lived in a trailer and liked to drink a whole lot. The only income he had was the crazy check that he received every month. Ever since he stripped down in a drunken rage and climbed the tower of the local radio station, claiming he was the Messiah.

He slipped off the bar stool and fell to his knees, slowly picking himself back up. "Okay, now I think I've had quite enough," he said. "Put it on my tab." He stumbled towards the exit of the bar.

"You might want to catch a cab, Jim," the bartender said.

"Now...what in the world would I wanna run after a cab for?" Jim walked out of the bar.

The cold city streets of the small town were slick with water and ice. Jim had a two mile walk make it home, where he'd probably drink some more.

Jim had become an alcoholic at the age of twenty-seven, when his wife left him for another man, his father. Up until then Jim was to inherit his father's hefty life insurance policy, six hundred thousand dollars. Jim was quickly dropped from the plan and his ex-wife was to inherit the money after his father died, which would turn out to be only a week later. Jim was broke, crushed, and had a nervous breakdown. The only thing he had to turn to was alcohol, he couldn't afford drugs.

Back at the trailer park, Jim's home, his brother, Melvin waited for Jim to return. Melvin was the more sensible sibling of the Varner family, ever since Jim's downfall.

Melvin was only a slight alcoholic, ten to fifteen beers a day, he'd only waste himself on the weekends. Melvin had a job as a windshield wiper at the local gas station, actually they just hired him because he'd never leave, he's a very lonely guy.

Jim was about a mile from home now as he stumbled along. He looked up only to see a big sign in the sky next to a convenient store that read *'Beer'*. Jim began to dig around in his pocket and pulled out a dollar and fifty cents. "Ah hah, just enough to get me another beer," he said as he stumbled through the door.

"Good evening, sir," the cashier greeted.

Jim walked to the back and quickly opened up the cooler, only to pull out a beer and take it up front.

"Are you drinking and driving, sir?" the cashier questioned.

"Dri...dri...drivin'? I sold my car for a bottle of rum...and a sammich." Jim threw his wadded up bill and coins on the counter and walked out.

Jim quickly drank his beer as he stood outside of the store, and then continued home. Stumbling and strolling along the side of the road, he fell to the asphalt of the road. As Jim looked up he saw the angriest, meanest, looking mutt that he had ever seen in his life.

The dog stood and growled at Jim as he struggled to get back to his feet. Foam now oozed from the dog's grizzly mouth, as he began to bark and snarl at Jim.

"H...hi...hi, little doggy," Jim said as he stood up and extended his hand to pet the dog.

The dog snapped at Jim's hand as he pulled it away just in time. "OH SH...," the dog bit into Jim's pants and ripped at them as Jim's fear now sobered him up and he started to run. The dog chased Jim out onto the nearby highway, where he began to kick at the dog, screaming for help.

A bright light came into focus as Jim turned his head in it's direction. It sped towards him as he continued to struggle with the dog. Jim ripped away from the dog's grasp on his leg and stumbled towards the oncoming light.

Jim threw his hands out...BAM!!! A cattle truck traveling eighty miles an hour down the highway hit him, without a clue...If you've ever seen what a watermelon looks like dropped from a twenty story building, you'd know about what Jim looked like after the truck had hit him.

The sun was up and the city cleanup crew was now scraping Jim's few and bloody remains from the highway with a shovel, putting them into a small plastic trash bag.

"Hey look," a cleanup guy said to another. "I found a nice watch wrapped around this piece of arm...or at least I think it's an arm," he pulled it off and stuck it in his pocket.

"Dude, you're gonna keep that?" another asked.

"Well, what's he gonna be needin' it for?"

They continued to scrape the remains from the road as the police searched the scene for any identification of the...body.

"Hey look, I found his wallet," one officer said to another as they stood at the side of the road. "No money." He threw it to the ground.

"Aren't you gonna check that for ID?" the other officer asked.

"Oh yeah." He picked it back up and opened it. "Jim Varner." He read off of a wrinkled up social security card.

The city cleanup crew was finishing up the job as the same dog that got Jim killed came out from some nearby bushes with a foot in his mouth and laid it at the foot of one of the guys. "Awww, look at the cute dog," he exclaimed, as he retrieved the foot and stuck it in his bag."

"Let's take him back with us," the other said.

The cleanup guys put the dog in the back of their truck and handed the bag of Jim over to the police.

Somewhere about three hundred miles away, a trucker stepped out of his vehicle to get a snack at the local mini-mart. As he walked to the front of his vehicle he noticed a large dent smeared with blood, "darn deer."

Jim's family gathered, well just his brother Melvin actually, to decide what to do with the...body. There was no way Jim was about to go into a casket, I mean, he had nothing really to fit into a casket. The only thing that could be done is either bury him in the trash bag he was contained in, or have him cremated. Since Melvin didn't like the idea of burying his brother in a trash bag, he decided it would be best to let Jim be cremated, and this is what was done.

Jim's ashes were placed in Melvin's most prized Tupperware dish, because he couldn't afford the urn. Melvin placed the ashes on his kitchen counter, so he could see his brother everyday he came home from work.

Since Melvin was so lonely without Jim around anymore and no friends of his own, he began talking to the ashes. He read them stories, slept with them, even took them to work with him.

Melvin's coworkers at the gas station soon teased him over his obsession with his brother's ashes. They teased him so much that he decided to go out one night to make new friends and leave his brother's ashes at home on the counter.

Melvin walked into the same bar that his brother had been in the night he was run over. He sat down at the counter next to a blind man with a wooden leg.

"How's it goin', partner?" The blind man greeted.

"Better than you," Melvin said under his breath as he ordered a beer.

Fifteen beers and three shots of Jack Daniels later, Melvin was wasted. Even if he had made any new friends he wouldn't have remembered.

Melvin stammered through his back door, holding the walls to keep him up. He gradually earned his balance and stood on his own two feet and began walking into the kitchen. He had a craving for coffee, he always liked to drink a cup of coffee after getting wasted, it sobered him out a little. He walked over to the counter looking around for the coffee grounds, but his head hurt so bad. Mistakenly, he opened up the Tupperware that contained his brother Jim and poured the ashes into the coffee filter. He brewed a hot cup of what he thought was coffee in a mug and sat down in his favorite chair...and took a nice long drink. *"This tastes funny,"* he thought to himself. *"Oh well."* He continued to drink, he drank it all to the last drop.

The early morning sun shining through the window onto Melvin's face woke him up out of his chair, still holding the coffee cup. He walked over to the sink where he put the cup and looked over at the Tupperware dish of unopened coffee grounds. *"That's strange,"* he thought to himself as he walked to the bathroom to take a shower.

Melvin sprayed Lysol on himself as he walked back into the kitchen, and was getting ready to go to work. He glanced over at his brother's ashes, only to see that they were missing. He thought to himself, *"Now what on Earth would anyone want to steal my brother's ashes for?"*

He glanced at the coffee grounds, then the cup, then the ashes, over and over again, thinking about being drunk last night. "OH MY GOD!!!" he screamed as he fell to his knees..."I drank my own brother."

Melvin was so tormented he didn't go to work. Not that day, the day after, or the day after that. He became bedridden as the horror of drinking his own brother overwhelmed him.

He lay in bed crying over the thought of the brother he used to admire as a kid consumed as a cup of brew, when all of a sudden he saw a ghost, the ghost of Jim. He looked angry as he walked towards the bed.

"B...bro...brother?" Melvin said as he cried.

"It is me, Jim," the ghost said.

"Did, you go to heaven?" Melvin asked

"Does it look like I'm in heaven?"

"Well, what are you back here for?" Melvin asked.

"I know what you did," Jim said.

Melvin pulled his covers up to his chin and gave a sad look, "you do?"

"You drank my ashes as a cup of coffee," Jim said.

"I'm so sorry," Melvin said. "It was a nice cup of brew though and I've been tormented ever since."

"I'm going to haunt you for the rest of your days," Jim said. "Unless you do this one little thing for me."

"Yes, please!" Melvin pleaded.

"I want you to take what's left of my ashes and bury them beside the highway where I was killed," Jim said.

"Why the highway?"

"Just...do it," Jim exclaimed as he disappeared.

Melvin almost wet himself over what he had just seen, but he hadn't drank anything in the past week, so he couldn't.

Melvin ran to the counter and picked up the Tupperware dish that had formerly contained the ashes of his brother. He looked and saw that there were still just a few left and ran out the door with them.

Melvin arrived at the highway about ten minutes later. The ground was wet, icy, and slippery. Melvin didn't want to throw the ashes out just yet. He stood there a while thinking about what he had done and everything else. He heard the sound of horns as he finally turned the Tupperware dish over and spread the few ashes on the highway. Melvin slipped on a patch of ice on the highway as he turned around to leave, only to meet his own demise, when a midget on a moped ran him down at sixty-five miles per hour.

You know, I'd usually just end the story here, but I'd bet a few of you'd be wondering whatever happened to those cleanup crew guys and that dog. Well, here's that story.

Eddy and Jack, the cleanup crew guys, were on their break messing around with the dog that they had taken back from the accident.

"Hey, what do you think we could feed it?" Eddy asked as they sat down eating at their desk.

"How about a cupcake?" Jack said as he opened one up and scarfed it down.

"Dogs can't eat cupcakes," Eddy said.

" but he does look really hungry," Jack said.

"Yeah, I know," Eddy replied.

The dog licked his snout as foam began to ooze from his mouth.

"He must want the cupcake Eddy, his mouth is watering up," Jack said.

"Fine, feed it to him," Eddy said.

Jack held the cupcake out to the dog who quickly snapped at it, but instead of getting the cupcake, the dog got Jack's arm.

"OH GOD!!!" Jack screamed as the dog bit into his arm and   began to play tug of war with it.

"Crap," Eddy grabbed a stapler off the desk and beat the dog in the head with it, the dog let go and Jack ran to the truck, then realized his keys were on the desk by Eddy and the dog.

The dog now ripped at Eddy's pants as he rushed for the truck.

Jack cried like a little girl as Eddy jumped on top of the truck screaming. The dog was barking loudly and began scratching at the truck door, Eddy too afraid to get off of the truck and run for help. No one ever saw those two again, but it sure was a cute dog.

THE END

2
Last Trailer On the RiGht

It was the night of All Hallows Eve. The dark, gloomy, sky as the black clouds races across the moon. The autumn leaves fell from the trees as a slight wind came through. The ground, dead and deserted of it's grass as the cold winter neared. The brown pond waters waded calmly in the air. A hooting owl in a tree made it's call all throughout the dark woods. POW! a gunshot sounded loud into the night.

"Woo hoo, I got me that there one!" Emmit, a hillbilly hunter from the backwoods of Grant, Oklahoma, said. "And that was my last bullet too." He put his pistol in his back pocket.

"Yeah, we can take it home and make a meal out of it. Cook it up with some good ol' ketchup, a bun, some tater salad, and a nice ol' gallon of milk to drink...even some mashed taters and ice cream for dessert. Now that there's some good eatin'," Hubert, his brother said. "Just make sure you get all the scales and the bones out. The last time I almost choked to death."

"Owls ain't got scales," Emmit said. "They got feathers."

They began to walk home through the silent woods, as the air suddenly started to get a lot colder.

"I can't feel my legs I'm so cold," Hubert said.

They walked up to *Bubba's Trailers,* the local trailer park they lived in. Sparks flew from the trailer park's neon sign as they walked into the basically empty lot, they called a trailer park, just four trailers, theirs the last on the left, and an old fireworks booth were there, 'cause hillbillies love fireworks.

Hubert walked ahead of Emmit to open the door of their trailer. "It's locked," he said as he tried to turn the knob.

Emitt held the dead owl in his hands. "Well, use your key you idiot, I gotta get this bird in the oven."

"I...I didn't bring my key," Hubert said.

"Oh, you're a real dummy...a real dummy," Emmit said. "Let's go over to one of the neighbor's to see if they know where momma went, so we can go get her to open the door."

They walked on over to the first trailer on the right, where the Manerberrys lived. Emmit still grasped the dead owl in his hands as Hubert began to knock. They waited a very long time, no answer.

They walked over to the second trailer on the right where the Hefburns lived. Hubert knocked on the door, again, and again, no answer.

They walked on over to the last trailer on the right. Jasper Filmore lived there, his wife Jodee had recently left him and he lived out his life in bitter sorrow, they didn't know him, seldom seen him, only when he went outside to put his cruddy garbage away. He was a strange man, often his shadow was visible as he sat in his chair by the front window. They had never ever talked to him before, out of fright, but if they were going to find their mom, tonight, this was their last choice.

Hubert walked up to 'DO NOT DISTURB' sign on the front door. "What's that say, Emmit? I can't read." He scratched his head.

"Hold on, let me sound it out," Emmit said. "Do...do...not...dis...dis...disturb," he read.

"What's disturb mean?" Hubert asked.

"Heck if I know," Emmit said, as he still held the owl. "It sounds like one of them five dollar school words. Just knock on the door, boy."

Hubert knocked on the door, no answer. He knocked again, still no answer. He knocked a third time...

BAM! The door flung open and Jasper held a rifle up to Hubert and Emmit from his doorstep. "If you're one of those gosh darned girl scout cookie sellers, I'm gonna blow you and them cookies back to hell where ya came from! And if you're trick or treatin' I ain't got no candy."

"No sir..." Hubert said nervously, "we came to see if maybe you know where our mother is."

"Well, I ain't got no answer for you, boy," he gave a grim and evil look. "And more certain, I ain't got no answer for you city folk...you make me sick!"

"City folk? We live in a trailer right across the park," Emmit said as he still held the owl.

Jasper looked at the owl and gave a toothless smile, "Is that a present for me?"

"No, this is dinner for me," Emmit said.

"C'mon let's go, Emmit," Hubert said. "Huh uh," Jasper said. "Y'all ain't 'bout to go nowheres, botherin' me's gonna cost you a lot more trouble, a lot more than you was lookin' for. Get in this trailer unless you wanna die," he aimed his gun at them, as they complied.

"See, I told you we should have dressed up like hillbillies and went trick or treatin' like the rest of the kids," Hubert said. "But no, you wanted to go huntin'."

"I'm not the idiot that forgot the key," Emmit said.

They walked into the old dusty trailer. It smelled of cigarettes and dead fish. The walls were all green and moldy. The whole place littered with cobwebs.

"Sit down," Jasper said as he pointed to an old brown couch, next to the door.

Hubert and Emmit sat down. "Man this place reeks," Hubert said.

"It's the smell of my mother, Jessie Sue Peggy Anne Robertson Ella Faye Buela Kay Johnson Jackson McDouglas Filmore, she was a hundred and ninety-seven years old. I buried her under the floor of the trailer. She talked too much. She had too many cats. And she dropped me on the head when I was a baby," Jasper said. "Father Time gave her a pretty good whoopin' himself...but I finished her off," he looked at his rifle and smiled.

"She sure had a lot of names," Hubert said.

"She sure had a lot of husbands," Jasper replied. "And I did away with them too." Once again glancing at his rifle he still wielded.

"What's your problem, man?...We just asked where our mom was," Emmit said as he still held the owl.

Jasper snatched the ol out of Ernest's hands and threw it out of an open window, by the couch. He then closed the window and locked it, "I'm tired of looking at that stupid thing," he said angrily. "Y'all keep on messin' with me and we're about to get rowdy up in here."

"That was my dinner though," Emmit said.

"Looks like it's my dog's dinner now," Jasper replied, as he licked his toothless gums.

"Listen...can we just go and you forget we ever bothered you?" Hubert pleaded.

"Oh no...you're not goin' anywhere." Jasper propped his gun against the wall and gave a wicked smile. "Tonight is the night of All Hallows Eve, the one night of the year when the dead can rise again. Mother is going to rise from her grave tonight, and mark my words, she will rise from the dead...and I'm sure she'll be hungry when she wakes up, and everyone knows the dead love to feast on the living."

"Well...well...I'm afraid we can't stay." Emitt said nervously as Hubert had a shocked look on his face. "You see, um...raising the dead is kinda against our religion...right, Hubert?"

"Uh, we ain't been to church in..."

Emmit nudged Hubert.

"Oh yes...of course," Hubert said, looking down nervously.

"Do you think I care?" Jasper said as he picked his gun back up, and walked to the back of his trailer. "You wait here, don't try to get away, 'cause that door's locked, and the window is too."

Emmit got up and grabbed a wrench he saw on the end-table, next to the couch., as Jasper was still away, he quickly stuck it in his pocket and sat back down.

"I'm scared," Hubert said.

"OKAY!" Jasper said. "HEEEEERE'S MOMMA!"

He wheeled the old decrepit figure into the room, hair still on her skull, and rotting stenches coming from her wreak old body.

"...She's still dead," Hubert said.

"Don't you talk about momma like that," Jasper said, as he pointed the gun at Hubert.

Emmit pulled the wrench from his pocket and bashed Jasper upside his head, knocking him to the floor.

Hubert broke the window with his fist and made his way out, he stood there waiting for Emmit, who came shortly after. They both stood there together looking at the trailer for a second.

Jasper poked his bleeding head out of the broken window.

"We're free now!" Hubert mocked Jasper, as they looked at him.

"I don't think so," Jasper said as he gave another toothless grin. "There's just one minor problem...turn around"

Emmit and Hubert turned around, there stood all of Jasper's mother's dead husbands...hungry for a meal.

THE END

3

Fartknuckle, Trailer Park
Of The Future

Somewhere in a galaxy, far far away, there is a place, a place in the dark, deep, aisles of space, roaming through the stars, not making a sound. After all, how could it since sound doesn't travel in space? This place is *Fartknuckle*, a trailer park space station. Where trailers still fill the land, and space, where rednecks still drink, where space wrasslin' is the most popular sports show on TV. Yes, it's an amazing place, well if you're a redneck anyway. No sun, no moon, only the stars to guide the way.

The year is 4015 A.D. The machines that man created have destroyed the Earth. The natural resources have all vanished. The surviving members of the human race have relocated to outer space, all living in large space stations. This is where our story begins.

Willy Frampton was walking back to his trailer, after getting off work from *Sleeze-E-Mart,* an intergalactic gas station. He had waited all day all day to get to his bottle of homemade moonshine he had won on Ebay, the last bottle of it from Earth.

Now the payment on Willy's trailer was a little overdue and he had been getting some nasty calls from the repossession agency. They had threatened to take his trailer away.

When Willy got to the place where his trailer was usually parked it wasn't there. All that was in his space was his, Ford Space-Ranger, spacecraft. "Now I know I was a little bit under the weather last night," Willy said to himself. "I musta left it somewhere else." He walked over to a neighbor's trailer and knocked on the door.

"Who is it?" a voice from inside asked.

"It's me, your neighbor, Willy," he answered.

The door slowly opened. "Whaddaya want?" an old lady in a robe, smoking a cigarette, asked.

"Do you by any chance were my trailer's at?" Willy asked.

"Oh, the Repo man came and got it about an hour ago."

"That son of a bi..."

"Said you're six months behind payments," the old lady interrupted.

"I gotta get that trailer back!" Willy said.

"Well, good luck," The old lady threw her cigarette down and closed the door, leaving Willy alone on the porch.

"I gotta get my trailer back," Willy said to himself. "I had my moonshine and my 'Space Booty' magazines in there," he walked to his Space-Ranger and got in. "I'll have to hunt him down," he attempted to start the Space-Ranger, but it wouldn't start. He tried again and again, nothing. Willy stepped out of the Space-Ranger and kicked the door. He sat down and thought for a moment. He decided to go to his best friend Bud's house to spend the night.

Willy walked to the nearby street and yelled for a Space-Taxi. One of the little yellow crafts stopped and

Willy got in. "I wanna go to West Main Apartments," Willy said.

West Main was on the other side of Fartknuckle, about thirty miles. The bad neighborhood of the space station, filled with prostitutes, drug lords, gangs, that was their turf.

Willy stepped out of the cab and onto the steel rusted streets of West Main. Broken down spacecraft lay in the junkyard in sight. The air smelled of tar and rust. It was dark and lonely.

"Hey papi, you want some good lovin'?" a scantily clad woman asked Willy as she walked up to him, obviously a prostitute.

"Good lovin'?" Willy said.

"You know..." She replied.

"Who are you?" he asked.

"By day, Dave Richards, at night, Fatima, the latin beauty."

"There ain't no day or night," Willy said.

"Oh c'mon," she...or it said.

Willy ignored her and walked toward the entrance of the *West Main Apartment Complex.*

"Hey buster," Willy turned around to see a large man pointing a gun at him. "Gimme all your money," he pushed willy to the metal ground below. Willy couldn't make out the man the place was too dark.

"I don't got any money!" Willy yelled.

"Willy?" the man said.

"How do you know my name?" Willy asked.

"It's me...Bud," the man answered.

"Bud?" Willy replied.

"Yeah, let's go into my place," Bud said. "I haven't seen you in a while."

They walked into Bud's apartment. Bud turned the

light on as Willy sat down on the dusty old couch.

"Why'd you try to rob me?" Willy asked.

"Well...I'm broke," Bud said. "I got laid off from the steel mill last week. It's the only way I can make any money."

"Oh, sorry man," Willy said. "I got my own little problem though."

What's that?" Bud asked.

"Repo-Man took my trailer," Willy said. "I'm six months late on payments. There's no way I can afford to get it back. I was gonna see if I could maybe stay here a while."

"How about we go steal your trailer back," Bud suggested.

"How in the world would we be able to do that?" Willy asked.

"We could go to the repossession agency's station" Bud said.

"That's like a light-year away," Willy said. "I gotta work tomorrow night."

"We'll be back by tomorrow afternoon," Bud said.

"You'll make it to work, my spacecraft's got a Hemi engine. I can go a quarter light-year per hour. We'll be there and back in about eight hours.

"I don't know..." Willy said. "What if we can't get it back?"

"We will...trust me," Bud said. "Besides, you ain't got nothin' better to do."

"True..." Willy said.

"Well, let's load up and get a scootin'," Bud said, as he grabbed a hat off an end table and put it on.

Bud started up his spacecraft as Willy stepped in and closed the door. "Let's roll," Bud said.

Bud started up the spacecraft and they started out on their adventure.

"What's the Repo-Man look like, Bud?" Willy asked.

"He's a big overweight fella," Bud said. "He's real greasy and gruff, smells like rotten cheese, eggs, and cabbage too."

They flew out of the vast realm of Fartknuckle and into the midst of the galaxy. They were warriors. Warriors prepared to do what no man had ever done before. They were determined to hunt down the Repo-Man to get that moonshine and 'Space Booty' magazines back...oh, and the trailer of course.

"Are we there yet?" Willy asked as he woke up in his seat for a light nap.

"NO, we still got three hours to go and I'm gettin' low on gas," Bud said. "I forgot to fill back up before we left."

"I don't wanna get stuck out here in space forever," Willy said.

"Huh oh," Bud said.

"Huh oh?" Willy said. "What was that Huh oh for?"

"Um...well," Bud said.

"Well what?" Willy asked. "We kinda ran out of gas and the engine kinda shut down..." Bud said.

"We ran outta gas," Willy said nervously. "WE RAN OUTTA GAS!!!"

"Don't go nuts there's a small planet down there we can land on," Bud said.

"Yeah and what if we can't breath down there? What if there's no air at all?" Willy asked.

"Well, in that case...we're screwed," Bud, answered.

"Oh great..." Willy said. "I sure have a whole lot to hope for now."

The spacecraft neared the small orange colored planet. "We're almost there but it's gonna be a rough landing," Bud said. They were speeding over the ground as the spacecraft came to a halting crash into the dirt of the small, orange, planet.

Willy crawled out of the mangled spacecraft. "I can

breathe," he said. "I'm alive!" he stood up and dusted himself off. "Hey, Bud, are you all right?"

Bud arose from the wreckage and sighed, "my vehicle...all broken and mangled, and I didn't even get to mud-dog in it yet."

"Well, at least we're alive," Willy said. "But now how are we gonna get out of here, get my trailer, and get back in time for me to be at work?"

"Don't ask me," Bud said. "I forgot to bring my telecommunicator."

"We'll have to find someway out of here...somehow," Willy said.

"Yeah...somehow," Bud repeated, as he looked into the blank red skies of the planet.

They walked along the sandy dunes of the dust, arid, land. The air was all hot and sultry. It felt like walking through hell.

"I don't think there's anyone out here," Bud said.

Willy walked around looking for someone or something. "Yeah me neither," he said to Willy, with a bland look on his face.

Bud noticed a small nearby cave and walked over to it, as Willy still searched the open land. He walked into the narrow opening. The space was dark. Bud hit something with his foot. He got down on his knees to see what it was, he couldn't make it out in the dark, so he decided to pull it out into the open light. "OH MY GOD!" He screamed as he noticed he was holding a human skull in his hands, along with the rest of the body down below. He dropped it in shock and stared down at the cold lifeless skeleton. "Willy, c'mere, look!" he yelled. Willy didn't come. He looked around "Willy?" he walked to the spot where Willy had previously been standing. As he gazed upon the land he heard a noise. He looked to where the noise was coming from. He saw two large, dark, men dragging Willy away in their muscular arms. "Oh man, I've got to get out of here," he said to himself.

"You're not goin' anywhere," a deep voice said behind Bud. He turned around to see what appeared to be a large native man clothed with animal hides and furs. He wielded a large club and struck bud with it quickly...

Bud awoke with Willy tied up next to him, they were each tied up to a large stake driven deep into the ground. No one else was around.

"Willy, wake up," Bud said, as Willy was knocked out. "WAKE UP!"

Willy woke up. "What is it? Where are we?" he asked.

"I don't know," Bud answered. "But I gotta take a pi..."

Just then about ten of the native men walked out all dressed with animal hides and furs. They untied Willy and Bud, who were both scared to death at this point. "What do you want from us?" Bud asked.

"We feast," a native said.

"Feast?" Willy said. "You have food?"

"We will," the native replied.

The men tied Willy's and Bud's hands together with a rope. "Walk," one of them said. "We taking you to feast."

Willy and Bud walked in the direction of the men as they were both in front and behind them, they had no chance of escape.

"Where do you think they're taking us?" Willy asked Bud.

"I don't know," Bud said. "But this seems like that night I spent in jail last New Years."

"What happened to you in jail?" Willy asked.

"Trust me," Bud said. "You don't wanna know."

They walked through a tunnel and came out the other end. There were more of these natives now looking at them. The men were all sitting down on the ground as the others forced Willy and Bud toward a large, round, smoking pot.

"So...what are we feasting on?" Bud asked one of the men.

"Beef stew," one of the men said.

Bud squeamishly looked down into the pot and saw carrots, tomatoes, potatoes, and onions all floating around inside. "Um...where's the beef?" he asked nervously.

The man smiled, "that's where you come in."

Bud gulped down the saliva that was stuck in his throat.

Willy started to cry. "Oh man," he wept. "I'm about to be some Indian's soup."

"Remove your clothes," the man said to Bud and Willy.

Bud looked at the pot again as steam began to rise and the water bubbled. Willy trembled.

"TAKE OFF YOUR CLOTHES!" the man demanded once again.

"Yep...just like that night in jail," Bud said, as he quickly bent over putting Willy on his back, since they were still tied together. Willy kicked the head native down as he went up and Bud ran as fast as a bat out of hell to get away. The rope miraculously broke and they were able to run together.

"Where we goin'?" Willy asked.

"I don't know," Bud said. "But if we go back there, we're gonna be the main course for those kooks."

Bud looked behind and saw the natives in the far distance, getting ready to come after them.

They were running out of breath, as they ran. The scorching heat had gotten to them. "I can't go on," Willy said as he fell to his knees. "I'm gonna die, save yourself."

Bud kneeled to the ground and pouted. "I'm sorry, I

shouldn't have come up with this dumb plan, it's all my fault."

"You're right" Willy said. "It is all your fault," he grabbed a handful of sand and threw it at Bud.

"HEY!!!" a voice called.

"Did you hear that?" Willy asked Bud.

"HEY!!!" the voice called again.

"Yeah, I hear it," Bud said.

They saw a small man rise up from behind a large rock. "C'mere," he said to them.

Willy looked at Bud, "Think he's one of them?"

"I don't know," Bud said. "but at this point...we have nothing to lose, we're gonna die anyway."

They walked towards the man. "Hello," he greeted. "My name's Jeffrey," he held out his hand.

"My name's Bud," Bud shook Jeffrey's hand.

"I'm Willy," he shook also.

"Are them Indian fellars after y'all?" Jeffrey asked.

"Yeah," Willy said.

"They are after me too," Jeffrey said. "I kicked one of them there fellars in the nads and ran. They're probably after all of us right now."

"Yep, they were gonna cook us," Bud said.

"Well, listen, my spacecraft crashed not too far from here, that's where I've been headed," Jeffrey said. "I'm pretty sure it still works, but those guys got me before I could fly off again. If you want to live and leave this place, you'll come with me."

"Well, I wanna live," Willy said. "I gotta make it to work tomorrow night or I'll get fired."

"You'll be dead, how can they fire you?" Bud asked.

They followed Jeffrey over the sandy, hot, terrain. Dust made sight less visible. The temperatures rose to miserable highs.

"You sure we're goin' the right way?" Bud asked Jeffrey.

"Yeah, we're almost there," Jeffrey said.

They walked though the dust winds until they saw an object in the distance, a GT79 Galaxy Cruiser.

"Here we are," Jeffrey said, as he opened the sand covered door of the cruiser.

"Looks like a hunk of junk," Willy said, as he stepped inside.

"What'd ya expect, it's a GT79," Jeffrey said. "All the way back from 3079 A.D."

"Yup," Bud reminisced. "I had one of these for my first ship, I was sixteen."

Jeffrey shut the door and started up the ship as Willy and Bud sat down.

"Hold on, I better fill up the gas tank," Jeffrey said as he stood up and got a can from the back. He opened the door and went outside, as Willy and Bud sat there.

"Okay, she's all filled up," Jeffrey said, as he stepped inside and put the can down. He went back to shut the shuttle door and was quickly snatched by one of the cannibal natives.

"OH MY GOD!" Willy yelled, as Bud ran over and shut the door and locked it. The hunters banged on the hard steel of the door.

Bud hopped in the driver's seat as they could hear Jeffrey screaming. He started up the craft, hit the gas, and took back off. They flew over the small orange planet and left it and Jeffrey behind.

"WOO! That was close," Bud said.

"Aren't we gonna go back and get Jeffrey?" Willy asked.

"Um...do you wanna die?" Bud replied.

Over the dark horizon of the blank space they could

finally see the Repo Agency's station in sight. They had finally made it to the destination they had been searching for all this time. They headed for the parking area of the station and landed there. Willy and Bud both stepped out of the GT79 onto the steel flooring of the parking lot...feeling like two real men.

"Ah, at last, we're here," Bud said.

"Yep, and I still think I can make it to work on time if we get my trailer back fast enough," Willy looked at his watch.

They walked in through large glass double doors into the main office. A little old red-headed lady, wearing glasses, sat there on the phone. "May I help you?" she asked with her nasal twain voice, lifting her ear from the phone.

"Yes, we're here to see the Repo-Man," Willy said, in a manly voice.

"I'm sorry, the Repo-Man's in a meeting at the moment, can I take a message?" she asked.

"DARNIT WOMAN!" Willy slammed his fists on the desk. "My friend Bud and I didn't travel all the way across the galaxy to hear no bull crap about takin' a message, now I want to see the Repo-Man and I want to see him now...you stankin' wench!" he eyeballed her down with a serious look.

The lady hung up the phone. "Sir, you're going to either have to let me take a message or wait, whichever you prefer."

Willy picked up a cup of hot coffee of the woman's desk and splashed it on her, she screamed in pain. "Now you tell the Repo-Man, I want to see him NOW! I want my trailer back, and I ain't leavin' 'til I get what I want, do you understand you old dust bag?"

Bud looked on in astonishment at Willy's anger as the woman stood up and walked away.

"You come back here you hussy and you tell me where my trailer is," Willy screamed at her, as she left.

They both took seats in the main office, as she hadn't yet returned.

A bald, greasy, overweight, man, wearing a small, white, t-shirt and raggedy blue jeans slowly walked in through the double doors. He burped loudly as the aroma of rotten eggs, cheese, and even cabbage came from him. "THE REPO MAN!" Bud said as he turned his head, getting a whiff of the guy's smell.

Willy jumped from his seat and tackled the overweight guy, quickly being thrown off.

"What's your problem?" the man asked.

"Are you the Repo-Man?" Willy asked as he got up.

"That'd be me," he let out some gas.

"Then you're my problem...you stole my trailer, I'm Willy," he said.

"Yes, and we've come all the way across the galaxy to get it back," Bud followed, as he stood up from his seat, scratching his head.

"You're six months behind payments," the Repo-Man said. "Pay your dues, and you can have your house back."

"I paid my dues in the Star Wars of 4010" he pulled up his pants leg, revealing a bionic limb. "Now I want my trailer back...now," Willy said.

"Yeah...now," Bud followed.

"Well, I don't think that's gonna happen," The Repo-Man said.

"Over my dead body," Willy said.

"Is that a challenge?" the Repo-Man asked.

"Sounds like a challenge to me," Bud said.

"I wouldn't let my friends speak for me if I were you, Willy," he said with his hot dragon breath, as Willy held his nose. "Is that a challenge?"

"Sure, why not?" Willy said.

"Then we shall duel...in my chambers, a light saber duel. You and your ignorant friend, against me, the almighty champion of the light saber," the Repo-Man said.

"And if we win?" Willy asked.

"You get your trailer back, of course," the Repo-Man replied. "But remember, I am a light saber champion, if I win, you die."

"Yeah," Bud whispered to Willy. "Keep in mind he IS a champion...C'mon Willy, please let's not do this. I just wanted to get out of the house. I'm gonna pee my pants I'm so scared."

"NO!" Willy said to Bud. "We didn't come all the way across the galaxy just to give up now."

"I...I...I did," Bud said. "AND WE AIN'T EVEN GOT NO LIGHT SABERS!"

"Don't worry," the Repo-Man said. "I'll supply you with one each."

"It's on," Willy said. "Us against you, fat boy," he gave a cold look.

Bud began to pray as the Repo-Man led them to his deep, dreary chamber room.

As they walked in to the dim old room, the Repo-Man gave them both their light sabers, which they quickly activated, ready to battle.

"Can't we just give up?" Bud said to Willy.

"NO!" Willy said as the Repo-Man activated his light saber.

Willy and Bud stood together, as the Repo-Man eyed the two of them down, ready to fight.

"Father, in your name I pray," Bud said as Willy jabbed him with his elbow.

"Let's duel," the Repo-Man said as he quickly came

after them swinging his light saber furiously, as they quickly tried to guard.

The Repo-Man slightly hit Bud in the side. "Ouch," he cried. "That really hurt," he struck the Repo-Man in the leg, in anger.

Willy jumped back as the Repo-Man's light saber brazed across his abdomen.

At this point they were doing more blocking than swinging, themselves. The Repo-Man was the fastest warrior either of them had ever seen, a true champion.

The battle waged on and on. Willy and Bud, fatigued from all the hasty blocking, they had to do. The Repo-Man was still going as strong as ever. It looked like there was no hope, but just to tire out and finally give up.

Things took a turn for the worst as Willy lost grip of his light saber and fell down in his broken tiredness.

Bud started running and screaming like a little girl, because he couldn't do it all by himself. The Repo-Man was walking towards Willy, as Bud screamed. He had his light saber pointed downward to strike Willy, while he was still down.

Willy quickly pulled his pants leg up and detached his bionic leg from the stump of his knee. He hopped up on one leg and quickly hopped across the room, distancing himself.

The Repo-Man walked nearer and nearer, with a grim smile upon his face, knowing he was about to defeat the two of them.

Willy quickly rose up his bionic leg and struck the light saber as the Repo-Man blocked.

"AH!!!!" The Repo-Man screamed as he backed away, dropping his light saber.

Willy closed in him, hopping, and wielding the leg. "Stay away," The Repo-Man said as he walked backwards.

Willy threw the bionic leg at the Repo-Man, who

quickly caught it, falling to the floor.

It seems the Repo-Man had a pacemaker and the radioactivity from Willy's bionic leg was interfering with it's system.

"AHHHH!!!" The Repo-Man said as he lay down...slowly dying.

Willy walked over to the Repo-Man, as Bud had settled down into a corner, crying.

"William, I have to tell you something," the Repo-Man said, as he slowly extended his arm out.

"Yes?" Willy said as he kneeled down to the body.

"William," he took a long breath. "...I am your father."

Willy looked on in astonishment as the Repo-Man closed his eyes and turned his head.

"Oh my god," Bud said, as he overheard.

The Repo-Man quickly turned his head and opened his eyes once more. "And your cousin, and your brother, and your uncle, and your grandfather, and even your brother in law twice removed," he closed his eyes in death.

Willy stood up, with a tear in his eye, as Bud got up from his corner and joined him. "I never knew my father," Willy said.

"By the way the trailer's parked out front," the Repo-Man said, still lying there, closing his eyes once more.

Willy and Bud made it all the way back to Fartknuckle, with a new perspective on life, and Willy's trailer.

Willy made it to work on time, and Bud went on home to watch old re-runs of, *I Was a Teenage Goat Lover*.

They both had found what they were looking for. Willy found his trailer and even his father. Whereas Bud found the adventure he had been looking for.

THE END

4

BreakDown

A sense of dread overwhelmed me as I entered the old trailer house.

"Hark, who goes there?" I heard a man say as he walked towards me.

He held a beer in one hand and a cap in the other. He wore no shirt, gleefully exposing his hairy, large, belly to the world.

"Cleatus? Cleatus, is that you?" he asked, as he placed the cap upon his head. "Cleatus, where ya been? I ain't seen ya in about twenty years."

Of course my name's not Cleatus, it's Jeb.

"Cleatus," he said again, as he stumbled ever so closer towards me. "Cleatus I believe you owe me some money," he said. Apparently this man was...drunk. For one, my name's not Cleatus. Also, I don't gamble...I steal. As he came even closer I started to back up as I recognized him, he was my preacher, from my old church. He had been thrown out of the congregation after he was caught embezzling the church building fund and using it to support his alcohol problem.

Why am I in this man's trailer, you ask? Well, my truck had broken down on the nearby highway. I had hoped to get home in time to watch wrasslin', there was a title match going on.

"Sir, my name's not Cleatus," I said. "I was hoping to use your phone."

"Oh, so now you're callin' me a liar?" he said, as he reached for something on a nearby table. He quickly pointed a carton of cigarettes at me, that he had taken from the table. "I don't appreciate you callin' me a liar." He said. "So I'm gonna shoot ya," he looked down at the carton of cigs and realized what he was holding. "Darn,' he said as he put them back on the table. "Let me go get my shotgun," he said as he walked to the back of the trailer.

I quickly scrambled to reach for the phone that lay on the table, beside the cigarettes. I proceeded to dial the number for the tow service as I heard two gunshots from the back of the trailer.

"Darnit Verna!" I heard the man yell in the back. "You been sleepin' with them there teddy bears again!"

I hurried into the room the man was in thinking he had done a gruesome deed. It was his bedroom that I found him in as I took a peek around the door. I quickly realized Verna was a blowup doll and hed had just fired the shots into her. He quickly turned his head and saw me in the doorway. "You been sleepin' with my Verna too, Cleatus?" he screamed at me, as he pointed the gun in my direction.

"Uh...uh...uh...I'm gay," I said, nervously. Of course I'm not gay, but that's about the only way I was going to get out of that.

"Oh really?" he said, as he gave a smirk. "Me too, Cleatus." He said excitedly as he dropped the gun. "I didn't know you rolled that way, Cleatus."

I rushed for the front door. If only I could get outside, I could make a getaway.

"Oh no, Cleatus, you ain't goin' nowhere," he said as he picked the gun back up and walked towards me. "I tell you what, Cleatus," he said he he came for me. "Either you pay me my money, or we're gettin' a little funny."

I had almost made it to the door, when I tripped over the telephone cord that ran through the room. He put the gun down. "Alright big boy, come to daddy."

I woke up in a bed...sweating, my head pounding. Oh no! What had happened!? Had I been?...I quickly jumped out of the bed, I still had my clothes on. I saw the man's gun on lying on the floor, I picked it up. I made my way around the bed and found the man, asleep on the floor, snoring like a baby.

I tried to creep out of the room without making a sound and waking the man up, but as I tiptoed something made strange sounds beneath my feet. I looked down. It was Verna's deflated body. The man started to wake up and noticed me leaving the room. "Cleatus, come back here." He said, as he hurried to get himself back up off of the floor. "Where's my gun.

I ran quickly to the phone to dial 911.

The man yelled, " We didn't even get the chance to foll around Cleatus, I passed out drunk, now come to papa."

I was relieved to hear nothing had happened, as I picked up the phone.

"I disconnected the line, boy," he said to me. "Did you really think I was gonna let you call the police or get outta here?"

I dropped the phone and went for the door. I made it! Only to find he had it locked from the inside.

The man pulled a key from his pocket and showed me he had it. "If I didn't think I'd choke on it, I'd swaller it, you surely couldn't get away then."

I noticed a clock on the wall. It was already 8:15 PM. OH NO! I was missin' wrasllin'! No tellin' who's gonna win that there title. With all my power and the strength within myself, I raised the gun at the man and pulled the trigger. Nothing happened.

"You really thought I had some bullets in there?" he snickered, as he waved a finger at me. "Tsk...tsk...tsk...not 'til deer season." I took the butt of the gun and jabbed him in the face three or four times with it, until he bled and fell to the ground, unconscious. I calmly sat down in his recliner, turned on the television and watched my wrasslin' as he lay out cold on the floor.

Later that night I called for a tow truck and was picked up, as

he still lay on the floor.

Last I heard, the guy who thought I was Cleatus. Well...I don't think he ever woke back up.

5

Christmas With Butch, Delray, and Al

Detroit, Michigan
The snow was falling on the slick city streets. The air was cold and misty. The streets covered in a thick cloud of snow with the heavy drooping branches of trees overhead. The holiday season was here and carolers were parading the streets singing joyous Christmas carols throughout the city's streets. Children building their snowmen in their yards and quarreling in snow fights. This was the time for reuniting. A time for peace, family, and giving. But this story's certainly isn't about peace, family, giving, or even Christmas carols. This story is my Christmas story.......

It was Christmas Eve at about 6 pm. Over at Al's house, Butch, Delray, and Al had finished exchanging gifts with each other and now Grandma Grechin, who was on the couch, was waiting for her gift from her son, Al. "I gotta special surprise for you momma," Al said, as he stood up off the rugged living room floor and walked into the hallway. "You got me a present?" Granny said. "But you never get me a present."

Al rolled a wheelchair into the room, which had a tiny blue bow placed on top. "Look momma," he said merrily. "I got you a wheelchair," he parked it in front of her. "Hop in," he said.

"What!?" Granny said with anger in her eyes.

"A wheelchair," Al smiled.

"You got me a wheelchair?" she said as she gave him the evil eye through her wrinkled face.

"Yeah, I thought you could use it," he said. "I mean you don't need to be walkin' around on that old cane momma, you can just wheel around now," he proceeded to take her cane, which was laying beside her on the couch.

Granny slapped his hand away. "So what you're sayin' is that you think I'm old huh?" she continued to eye him down. "What you're sayin' is I cant get around all by myself."

"Momma, I just thought it'd be easier for you to get around," he said.

Butch and Delray sat on the floor, watching. "This is gonna

get good," Delray said as he got up and pulled two beers out of the ice chest beside them and opened it.

"It sure is," Butch took a beer from Delray and opened it, as Delray had already started gulping his down.

"So you think I'm gettin' old right?" Granny said to Al.

"Well momma, you're 97 years old, and you're not gettin' any younger," he replied.

Granny rose up from the couch. "97 years old, huh?" she picked up her cane and grasped it strongly within her hands. "I'll show you 97 years old, you little......"

"Now momma, get a hold of yourself....," Al took a step back.

Butch and Delray walked into the kitchen where they could see the fight without getting whacked by Granny. Granny swung the cane at Al's bald, greasy, head and

40

knocked him down. "You fat loser," she said, as she watched him fall.

"Ow momma, that hurt," Al stood up, rubbing his head.

She hit him upside the head again which knocked him clear across the room. Butch and Delray stood in the kitchen laughing. Grandma Grechin picked up the wheelchair and pitched it through the living room window. The window shattered and the wheelchair flew over the porch and landed in the dirt of the front lawn.

Terrance, the neighborhood thief, was walking by as the wheelchair hit the ground. He picked up the wheelchair and looked at it for a moment. "Oh yeah," he said, as he sat down in the seat of the chair. "Now I gotta reason to draw me some disability," he smiled. "Nobody ever thought I'd make it, but with me livin' of the gov'ment it's all good," he rolled down the street.

Back in the house, Butch, Delray, and Al put their coats on and were walking out the front door as Granny was still griping about the wheelchair. They walked out the door into the icy, polluted, streets of Detroit. "You know," Butch said. "That beer didn't do the trick for me, I need some hard liquor."

"Yup, me too," Delray said.

"Uh huh," Al followed.

They walked to the front of 'Ray's Liquor Store'. "It's actually open on Christmas Eve," Butch said. "I can't believe he's not out huntin' or somethin'," he opened the door and they all walked in.

Fat Mac was sitting in a chair dressed like Santa Claus with a red velvet suit and a white fuzzy beard he was drinking a forty ounce bottle of malt liquor. "What's up, homies?" he slurred through his drunken speech. "Wanna get high......?"

"Shut up," Ray said to Fat Mac. "What do you boys

need?" he asked Delray.

"Some good, hard, liquor," Delray said. "Three bottles of it."

"Gonna drink on the day before Jesus' birthday," Ray said. "Y'all goin' straight to hell."

"I ain't goin to hell," Fat Mac said as he still sat down, unable to get up from his intoxication. "Jesus made water into wine, so what's wrong with drinkin' a lil' bit just to celebrate the savior's birthday?"

"Shut up," Ray said, as he handed Butch, Delray, and Al their liquor and Delray paid.

Fat Mac stood up and stumbled out ahead of Butch, Delray, and Al. "I'm goin' to church," he mumbled.

"Well, at least you're doin' somethin' good," Ray said.

"Shoot......," Fat Mac said. "I'm gonna go smoke it up with

the preacher," he left the store.

Ray shook his head, "I don't know about that boy. Where are y'all headed anyway?" he asked Delray.

"Well, certainly not back to Al's house," Delray answered. "His momma's gone nuts," he adjusted his trucker cap.

They walked out of the liquor store with the bottles of liquor in hand. "What are we gonna do?" Butch asked.

"I don't know," Delray said.

"Maybe we could go to church," Al said.

"Church?" Delray said. "What are we gonna go to church for?"

"I only went to church once," Butch said as he drank his liquor. "And that was when I mistaked it for a bar."

"How in the world do you mistake church for a bar?" Delray asked.

"I was pretty drunk," Butch said. "Like I am now," he scratched his head.

They walked into the 'Third Church of Jesus Christ'.

"Man, we ain't even dressed for this," Delray said, as he drank his liquor, walking toward the sanctuary.

"You can't have liquor in God's house," Al said, as he and Butch walked beside Delray.

"Ah..... this ain't God's house," Delray said as he drank some more. "It's paid for by the government, I can do anything I want, not my fault you dummies drunk yours already," he walked into the sanctuary and sat in a pew near the front row beside Fat Mac, who was still heavily intoxicated and wearing his Santa suit with the beard. Butch and Al followed, as the sermon had just started.

Reverend Washington stood in front of the large crowd of church-goers and began to preach.

"Salvation......," the reverend said. "Salvation.... God shall give you salvation, as long as you give to God," he wiped the grease that dripped from his Jeri curl off his forehead with a cloth and continued. "I feel the holy spirit in this room," he said. "Now I see, I see that we have some sinners among us," he shook his head. " But today, we are having a special on sins. I say you can get two sins forgiven for the price of one. THAT'S RIGHT ladies and gentleman, two sins for the price of one. Just ten dollars and you can be forgiven for two sins, write your name down and we'll give you a FREE bottle of miracle healing water for a small donation of twenty dollars also. It heals everything from arthritis to hemorrhoids. Now remember, you have to give to God to receive from God!" He looked towards the crowd and smiled. "Now Brother Jenkins will be passing around the offering plate durin' this period of time. Give to God and he shall spare your soul from the lake of fire, eternal damnation, the fiery bowels of hell. Yes, money is the way, the gateway to heaven. Be sure to give all that you can. God doesn't run heaven for nothin' now." He walked towards the exit of the room. "Now I'm gonna take a ten minute break while y'all finish givin' to the lord." He left.

"Shoot, he goin to smoke some," Fat Mac said. "Do it every church night," he pulled a cigar from his pocket. "You see, I'm proud to be a dope fean though," he said. "I don't care what y'all think of me," he smiled. "I'm gonna fire it up right here and now," he lit up his cigar and took a puff. "Want some?" he asked Butch, Delray, and Al.

"Nah," they all said.

"Ahhhh......," Fat Mac screamed as he got up and jumped into the aisle.

"Guess the holy spirit got a hold of him," Al said.

"My beard's on fire!" Fat Mac screamed as he patted the fire out and threw the beard to the floor. He took a last puff of his cigar and put it out on the arm of the pew. "Man, that shocked me so bad, I'm all sobered up," he shook his head. "I ran outta liquor," he walked out of the church.

"Man, I ain't stayin' here neither," Delray said, as he stood up from the pew and walked towards the lobby, still drinking from his almost empty bottle of liquor. Butch and Al got up also and walked out with Delray. They walked out of the lobby and outside.

"Hey, y'all ain't s'posed to be out here," Reverend Washington said as he threw a joint down and quickly stomped it out on the concrete sidewalk. "What was that?" Butch asked

"That's for my Glaucoma, don't you go tellin' nobody neither," he stared at Butch. "Or you shall be thrown into the eternal lake of fire," he walked back into the church singing James Brown tunes as he ran his hands through his greasy jericurl.

Delray took the last sip of his liquor and dropped the bottle to the concrete, as it broke to pieces.

"Hey, you ain't s'posed to do that," Butch said.

"Ahhhhhh, who cares?" Delray said.

"Jesus cares," Butch said.

"This ain't Jesus' place, it's owned by the government, like I said," Delray said as he walked into the parking lot, towards the road, Butch and Delray followed.

"BOO!" a voice said behind Butch, as he sprang forward in fright, screaming loudly. He turned around to see what it was.

"Fat Mac?" he said.

"HaHaHa," Fat Mac laughed. "You scream like a girl," he gently pushed Butch. "Where y'all headed to now?" he asked, as he started walking with them.

"Don't know," Delray said. "I'm walking back to the trailer park." He adjusted his trucker cap as he walked.

"Yeah, me too," Butch said.

"I gotta be home by 12, momma said so," Al said.

"What you gotta be home by 12 for?" Fat Mac asked.

"Santa Claus won't visit me." He shrugged his shoulders. "You mean to tell me you don't believe in Santa Claus?" He looked at Fat Mac.

"I'm 35 years old, Al," Fat Mac said. "And you're 43, you should have better since than that," he laughed.

"You're just jealous 'cause you ain't gettin no presents, you been a bad boy," Al said as he looked at his watch. "Darn, it's only nine," he said. "Guess I'll go to the trailer park with y'all," he said.

They walked up to the front of the trailer park. "Delray's Trailer Park Emporium," the weathered sign read above them.

"Yep," Delray said. "25 years in the business." He hit the pole that held the sign up. The whole sign fell down behind them, hitting the dirt of the ground. "Darn termites." He walked toward his trailer. Tuck, his dog was growling at them all like crazy. "Ever since he got bit by that 'coon last week he's been actin' funny," Delray said, as he looked up and noticed Jackie's truck parked outside his yard.

"What's she doin' here?" Butch asked.

"I don't know," Delray said as he walked up the front steps of his trailer and opened the door and he, Butch, and Al walked inside to 12 kids going through Delray's things and putting them into large plastic sacks.

"WHAT IN THE!!!!!!!" Delray yelled. "WHAT'S GOIN' ON HERE?" he screamed.

Delray Jr. walked up to him and said, "Momma told us we could go through your things and take whatever we wanted, and that'd be our Christmas gifts from you."

"Where's your momma?" Delray asked him.

"She's in the truck," Delray Jr. said.

Delray stammered out the door towards Jackie's truck, as Butch and Al stayed inside and sat on the couch, watching as the kids stole Delray's things.

"What are you doin' Jackie!?" he yelled at her as he talked to her, through her rolled down window.

"Well, you don't pay no child support and you never get them kids anything, so I figured it was time you started," she said to him.

"Them ain't my kids!" he yelled. "They could be anyone's kids," he said with anger. "Anyone in the county," he took a step back from the truck. "You got five seconds to get those kids outta my trailer!" He looked at her.

"No," she said, as Delray counted.

"3.... 4..... 5....," Delray walked towards his trailer and grabbed a shovel.

"You're just bluffin'," she yelled out of the truck window.

He walked into his trailer with the shovel and said, "You little punks got 5 seconds to get outta here before I start takin' you out!" He started counting again as the kids didn't listen to him, "1......2......3......4......5, alright, y'all didn't listen I gave you the warnin'," he threw the shovel down and opened the window and started pitching the kids out of it onto the ground 7 feet below until they were all out.

"My momma did that once to me," Butch said. "I was six months old and I landed on my head," he said. "Maybe that's why I'm so...so.... what's the word I'm lookin' for?" he scratched his balding head.

"Stupid?" Al said.

"Yeah..... Stupid," Butch said.

Delray walked outside the trailer and all 12 kids had rocks in their hands waiting for him. "Hey what are y'all?!?!" before he knew it he was bombarded by rocks from all 12 kids, he was screaming bloody murder as every rock hit him. He stumbled down to his dog, Tuck, as the kids reloaded on rocks. They threw more rocks at him as he made his way to the dog, he dodged most of those and was hit by a few. He made it to the dog and released him. "Get 'em Tuck!" he yelled as he let the rabid dog go.

"Delray Gibson, what are you doin?" Jackie yelled out of her truck window, as the kids were now running for their lives and hopping in the back of the truck.

Tuck caught one of the kids by the leg and he was now screaming for help. "Hahahahaha..." Delray laughed and pointed. "Get 'em Tuck, Get 'em boy," he said.

Jackie got out her Truck and kicked the dog off her kid. "Hey, that's my prized huntin' dog," Delray said.

"Well your prized dog probably just gave the kid rabies," she picked her son up off the ground and put him in the truck. "I'll be mailin' you a doctor bill," she got in her truck and quickly drove off.

Delray tied tuck back up and stumbled back into the trailer. "I wonder why that darn dog's foamin' at the mouth," he wondered to himself. "It was probably just some bad puppy chow." He shrugged, as he sat down with Butch and Al.

"Why are you so beat up?" Butch asked.

"Those darn kids hit me with rocks," Delray answered.

"Ha," Butch laughed.

"Well, I better get back home" Al said, as he stood up and walked towards the door. "It's past eleven and it'll take me twenty minutes to walk home," he walked out the door and waved bye to Delray and Butch. "Well, I guess that leaves all the booze to us," Delray said as he got up and pulled two beers from the refrigerator.

"Yup," Butch said, as Delray handed him a beer and sat back down. "So, what are you doin' tomorrow for Christmas?"

"Well, I imagine I'll do what I usually do," Delray said.

"What's that?" Butch asked.

"Drink," Delray said. "Ain't nothin' better than drinkin' on Christmas."

"Cheers to that," Butch said, as he raised his can of beer.

"Cheers," Delray said.

THE END

6

Rednecks In Hawaii

The air was crisp and sweet. A light breeze blew as the sun shone over the green rolling hills of the meadow. It wasn't too cool, not too warm, just the right feeling. It was almost paradise. In fact...it was paradise.

Clem mowed the grass with joy as it was the most beautiful day he had ever seen. He was mowing with the most beautiful mower he had ever seen.

Suddenly the most beautiful girl appeared out of nowhere. She had the most voluptuous body Clem had ever gazed upon. All her curves were in the right places, small waist, no fat, the most immaculate bosoms and a tight derriere you could sleep on. She wore a beautiful red tube top and blue jeans that grabbed her rear tighter than a fat kid hiding his cupcake. She had the waviest long locks of blonde hair. She was the angel of his eyes. She pulled a beer from behind her and held it to him as he was closing in ever so nearer. He had just gotten to her when...

"Clem!!! Clem!!! Wake your sorry butt up!" Clem rose up to see his friend, Ed, shaking him. "We got lost at sea and ended up on some strange island...or somethin'."

"Where are we?" Clem asked. "What happened?"

"I dunno," Ed answered. "We were at the fishing tournament in California and got swept off to sea in a storm...and you fell asleep...and the boat's got a hole in it."

The sun was bright in the sky, shining down on the palm trees and beach below. Tropical birds roamed the air as the beautiful, blue sea waters. This was the beautiful and luxurious Hawaii, but Clem and Ed wouldn't know that.

Clem and Ed stepped out of their small wrecked fishing boat onto the sandy beach.

"Yep," Clem said. "I reckon we're lost." They walked along the sandy, abandoned beach, making their way to a bushy area. They slowly walked through the large amount of bushes, leading them to a crowded city street.

"What in tar nation?" Clem said.

"I dunno..." Ed said. "But it sure ain't the trailer park."

"I've never seen so many buildings without wheels," Clem gazed upon the large buildings and fancy houses.

Natives and tourists filled the streets. Clem and Ed had to be the two most confused rednecks ever.

"What's your explanation of this, Clem?" Ed asked.

"We musta died an' gone to Hell, Ed, ain't a truck or trailer nowheres in sight," Clem answered. "What do you think, Ed?"

"Well, I don't know," Ed answered. "But I sure could use a cold beer right about now."

"You ain't the only one, Ed, you ain't the only one."

Ed stopped one of the guys that walked along the city street, "do you mind tellin' a fellar where he is?" "Honolulu," The man said.

Clem looked at the man. "Honolulu? Where in the Hell is that?"

"Hawaii," the man said. "Beautiful Hawaii." He walked on away.

"Well, if it ain't Hell, it's Hawaii." Clem said.

Ed pulled a cassette tape from his pant's pocket. "You reckon they got anywhere I can listen to some Merle Haggard?"

Clem snatched the tape and looked at Ed with disappointment. "We're stuck millions of miles from home and all you wanna do is listen to Merle Haggard?" Clem stuck the tape in his pocket. "Besides Garth Brooks is much better, you loser. By any chance do you have some money?"

"No," Ed said. "All mine's back in California. Why do you ask?"

"Well, I thought we could use a pay phone, or buy a beer," Clem said.

They continued walking along the sidewalk, the sun glistening in the clear blue sky. Clem bent down and picked up a round, shiny, object, "it's a quarter...we could call somebody."

"Yeah," Ed said. "We could call cousin Cleatus."

"Cousin Cleatus!?" Clem yelled. "What's cousin Cleatus gonna do about this?"

"Well, he's a chicken farmer," Ed said. "I figured he could send us some chickens so we wouldn't starve while we was down here."

Clem slapped Ed in the back of the head, "You idiot!" he yelled. "We're tryin' to get outta here, not stay."

"I'm tellin' Ma you hit me when we get home," Ed said.

"Look, dummy, now I got a plan," Clem said.

"Oh and what's that?" Ed asked.

"We call the immigration on ourselves, the deportation," Clem said. "They'll deport us outta here, we just tell 'em we're Mexican...free transportation. I think it's possibly the most genius idea I've had since we sold your body for new lawn furniture."

"But I didn't make but nine dollars," Ed said. "And that was from that old lady down the street that likes to give me cookies."

"Doesn't matter...you're just jealous 'cause you didn't come up with it," Clem said. "Now this is gonna work, it's fool proof. I'm tellin' ya."

"So you really think it's gonna work?" Ed asked for reassurance.

"I'm certain," Clem said as he looked at the quarter. "All we gotta do now is go and find ourselves a darned payphone."

They walked along in the tropical heat. They got on the nearest sidewalk and walked up to the first payphone that they could find.

Clem put the quarter in the coin slot as he picked up the phone.

"Do you know the number to immigration?" Ed asked.

"Darnit..." Clem exclaimed. "I just realized...I...I...don't know." He began to pull the change return tab to get a second call, but his quarter would never come back, he pulled and pulled and never got anything. "DARNIT! DARNIT! DARNIT!" He yelled in frustration, as he slammed the phone up against it's base.

"Well...I guess now's not the best time to tell you that if you hadn't hung up the phone...the operator would have come on and you could have gotten the number from her?" Ed asked.

"What happened to you during birth, Ed? Did they wait too long to spank you and make you breathe?"

"Actually, I was dropped on my head...more than once," Ed answered.

"Okay, we're broke, I'm scared to ask one of these crazy looking people for a quarter, and you're just...stupid," Clem said. "So it looks like it's all downhill from here."

"I'm not stupid...I'm remedial...don't you remember those classes I had back in high school? REMEDIAL...I'm tellin' Ma," Ed said.

They sat down on a nearby bench as tourists and natives still walked the street in the hot sun. The sun bore down upon them as they sweat. All either of them wanted to do was just go home. They couldn't find the luxury of Hawaii. They liked their little trailer on the coast of their small town in Southern California. Now they were stuck in Hell, as they sat there thinking of a way to maybe get out, somehow to just get back home.

"I GOT IT!" Clem said.

"Got what?" Ed asked.

"I know where to get a quarter!?" A grim look appeared upon Clem's face as he looked at Ed. He gave a devilish smile, growing every second.

"Where you gonna get a quarter?" Ed asked.

"See that hobo over there?" Clem pointed to a small gray haired, toothless, man holding out a cup for donations on the corner across the street. "I'll walk up to him and act like I'm about to give him some money and you tackle him...just knock him down to the ground, I'll do the rest."

"Hello..." Clem said to the man. "How are you this fine day?"

The old man smiled and held out the cup to Clem, and in that exact moment he was pummeled to the ground by Ed running and jumping on top of him. He dropped his cup and Clem picked it up. As the hobo still lay hurt on the ground, Ed walked up to Clem, who had just dug a quarter out of the cup.

"I've got what we need," Clem said, as they began to walk fast down the sidewalk.

They made their way up to the payphone they had been at a while before. Clem picked up the receiver and placed it to his ear, while putting in the quarter, and waiting for the operator.

"Operator..." a woman said on the other end of the line, shortly.

"Yeah...we'd like to report some Mexicans," Clem said.

"What do you mean?" The operator asked.

"Umm...Mexicans...they like are illegal and stuff, no cards, no documents, no English, we need them picked up...I feel in danger," Clem said.

"I'll have to report it to deportation," the operator said.

"Yeah," he looked at himself and what he and Ed were wearing. "Um...they've got on some dirty overalls and trucker hats...they look kinda like white guys...but they're Mexican I tell ya."

"Okay," the operator said. "You keep them there and I'll have the INS over shortly."

"Alright," Clem said. "We've got them Mexicans over here. You're tracing the call right?"

"Sure am, I know where it is," the operator said.

Ed stood by the phone looking stupid...as usual, as Clem hung up the phone.

"We're gonna be outta here in just a little while," Clem said.

INS agents showed up shortly, capturing Clem and Ed, who pretended to know no English. They were board upon a plane and shipped out of Hawaii. They thought they were on their way back home and both had smiles on their faces, thinking they had just gotten a free ride. But when their plane landed and they got off...they were placed in handcuffs and read a sign, "*Welcome To Tijuana.*"

THE END

Printed in the United States
44726LVS00006B/190-219

9 781424 105670